ARE YOU CURIOUS TO LEARN MORE ABOUT YOUR FAVORITE PET!

THERE IS SO MUCH TO KNOW!

Pet rabbits are fascinating! They can be adorable and energetic, making them great pets for children and adults alike.

Rabbits and bunnies
are the same animal
there's no difference
in breed or species,
just the word we prefer.

Each time a female
gives birth she will
have from three to eight babies.
Baby rabbits are called
'kits' or 'kittens'.

A female rabbit is called a Doe.

A male rabbit is called a Buck.

Rabbits are mammals.
A group of rabbits is called a warren.

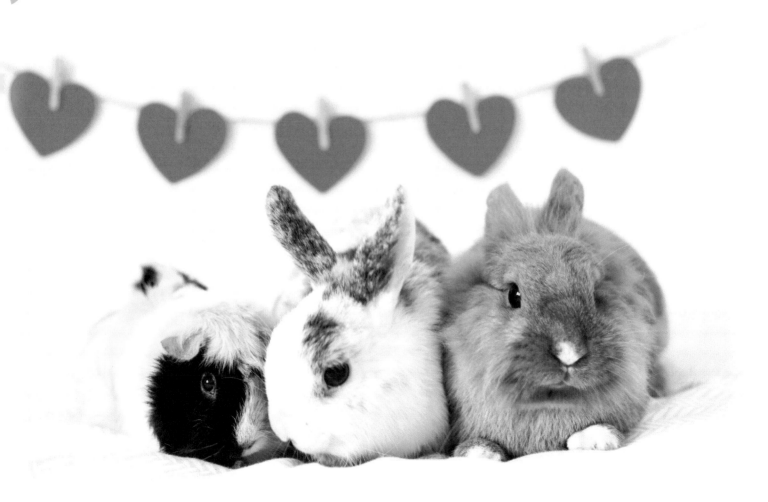

Did you know that more than half of the world's population of rabbits actually live in North America. And island of Japan called Okunoshima is occupied by wild rabbits. Because there is no predators on this island they are free to roam the forests and the paths.

Rabbits are meticulously clean animals and are easy to house break and train. Much like a dog, a pet rabbit can be taught to come to his/her name, sit in your lap, and do simple tricks.

A baby rabbit will stay with his
mom for about two weeks.
This is a very short period of time
after which they have to fend
for themselves.

🐰 A rabbit can live up to 10 years.

🐰 On average, they sleep about eight hours a day.

🐰 Rabbits have short tails.

🐰 Rabbits cannot vomit!

NOT TESTED ON ANIMALS

A rabbit symbol
is often used to show
that a product was
not tested on animals.
This is because rabbits
have traditionally been
used in product safety testing.

Rabbits will not start having babies
until they are about one year old.
On average they can have about
25 babies in the year which is amazing.

Rabbits have long ears and on average can be 4 inches long.

A mother rabbit feeds her kids for just about five minutes a day.

They are social, playful pets. It's important to keep bunnies entertained with plenty of toys, chews, and attention. We also recommend interacting with your bunny with treats, petting, and more.

The rabbits can make sounds that are very similar to that of a cat.

Rabbits start breeding at an early age, when they are three to four months old!

When a rabbit is happy they jump and twist which is named as "binky".

Rabbits are amazing
athletes they can jump
as high as 90 centimetres
in one leap!

The droppings of a rabbit are widely used as a fertiliser in gardens.

Rabbits easily suffer
heat stroke and therefore
prefer to live in cool places.

With their eyes placed
wide apart they can
easily see behind them.

There are four
types of fur
Normal, Rex, Satin,
and Angora fur.

rabbits can turn
their ears by 180 degrees,
keeping a careful listen
out for predators.

They typically have one of
five eye colors brown, blue-gray,
blue, marbled, and pink.

rabbit that lives
in doors is normally
called a house rabbit.

There are currently 45 known breeds of rabbits

The meat of a rabbit
is not red but white.

Printed in Poland
by Amazon Fulfillment
Poland Sp. z o.o., Wrocław

64211611R00019